KNIGHTSHAYES COURT

Devon

THE NATIONAL TRUST

Acknowledgements

The National Trust is very grateful to the late Joyce, Lady Heathcoat Amory for providing an abundance of information on both the house and the garden. Carola Stuart and the late Michael Trinick each contributed the fruits of their research on the early history of the Knightshayes estate, and Michael Hickson was especially helpful on the recent history of the garden. Alastair Laing revised the picture entries and contributed the introduction to the paintings in the Drawing Room.

Hugh Meller, 1999

Further Reading

Megan Aldrich, ed.: *The Craces: Royal Decorators, 1768–1899*, Brighton, 1990, pp. 114–20; J. Mordaunt Crook, *William Burges and the High Victorian Dream*, London, 1981, pp. 302–5; 'Knightshayes, Devon: Burges versus Crace', *National Trust Year Book 1975–76*, London, 1976, pp. 44–55; W. Gore Allen, *John Heathcoat Amory and his Heritage*, London, 1958; Sir John Heathcoat Amory, 'A Garden in a Wood: Knightshayes Court', *Journal of the Royal Horticultural Society*, lxxxv, October 1960, pp. 431–9; Arthur Hellyer, 'Out of the Wood', *Country Life*, 8 March 1990, pp. 80–5; Barbara Keene and Dot Butler, *Knightshayes Court from Knightenhaie to National Trust*, Tiverton, 1997; D. E. Varley, *John Heathcoat*, Newton Abbot, 1968.

© 1981 The National Trust

Reprinted 2002 (twice), 2004, 2006, 2007, 2008, 2009;
revised 1984, 1986, 1989, 1990, 1992, 1996, 1997, 1998, 1999, 2003, 2005

Registered charity no. 205846

ISBN 978 1 84359 058 3

Photographs: National Portrait Gallery, London p. 43; National Trust pp. 10, 22, 27; NT/Nicholas Toyne p. 6 (top right); NT/Chris Vile p. 12; National Trust Photographic Library pp. 11 (bottom left), 16, 18, 28, 29, 46; NTPL/John Bethell pp. 6 (bottom left), 11 (top right); NTPL/Prudence Cuming p. 30 (bottom); NTPL/Andreas von Einsiedel front cover, pp. 14, 15 (top and bottom), 17, 20, 23, 24 (top and bottom), 30 (top), 31; NTPL/John Hammond pp. 1, 4, 6 (top left), 19, 26, 40, 41, 42, 44, 45, 48, inside back cover; NTPL/Angelo Hornak p. 47; NTPL/Stephen Robson pp. 5, 7, 34, 35, 36, 37, 39, (back cover); NTPL/Rupert Truman pp. 8, 9, 33.

Designed and typeset from disc by James Shurmer (08 08)

Printed by BAS for National Trust (Enterprises) Ltd,
Heelis, Kemble Drive, Swindon, Wilts SN2 2NA
on Cocoon Silk made from 100% recycled paper

(*Front cover*) The Library ceiling, which features Burges's characteristic gilded 'jelly-mould' domes

(*Title-page*) Burges's design for the north front. The great tower was never built

(*Back cover*) The Pool Garden

CONTENTS

LIVING AT KNIGHTSHAYES COURT

by Joyce, Lady Heathcoat Amory

It is now getting on for 50 years since I married and came to live at Knightshayes. At first sight I remember a feeling of some alarm at the prospect of living in this big house, but I can only say that over the years it has become a much beloved home, giving out a warm and welcoming atmosphere to all who visit it. I attribute this largely to the fact that Knightshayes, very much a family home, has always been lived in all the year round, and never left empty and desolate for parts of the year, as happens to so many large houses. The Amory roots were well buried in Tiverton.

Perhaps it would be as well to admit at once that the Heathcoat Amorys were from early days unable to appreciate Victorian architecture, even though Knightshayes was built by a very distinguished Victorian architect. Each generation has played its part in dismantling the most eccentric and ornate features in the house. The National Trust, since taking it over in 1973, is patiently and with dedication, as circumstances permit, restoring the lost workmanship of Burges and Crace.

The old house played its part in the two world wars; in the first as a Red Cross Hospital, and in the second beginning as a hastily organised Casualty Clearing Station in the event of possible invasion, but eventually ending up as a Rest Home for US airmen. Very near the end of the Second World War a sad tragedy took place. It was the custom for departed occupants to return from their airfields in order to 'buzz' the house, which meant flying up the park almost at tree level, to applause and clapping from the terrace. One fighter pilot, alas, lost his life, his plane hitting the tops of several trees. The clearing away of the broken trees after the war was, more happily, the beginning of the 'Garden in the Wood'.

I can write only about the years my husband and I lived together at Knightshayes. Although we must bear our share of 'vandalism', some of the Victoriana we destroyed between 1950 and 1970 was for the purpose of providing a suitable background for a small but very fine collection of Old Masters. It was understood that any purchase had to be approved together, which made it such an absorbing interest for both of us. We began soon after the war in a very modest way, the collection growing over the next twenty years, fortunately before prices increased astronomically. The pictures finally chosen were widely selected. One of the earliest is the very beautiful sixteenth-century

Joyce, Lady Heathcoat Amory; by H. N. Wethered (Golf Room)

*Lady Heathcoat Amory and her husband created the
Garden in the Wood in the 1950s and '60s*

Nativity by Lucas Cranach, and the nineteenth
century is represented with paintings by Constable,
Bonington and Turner. This is a collection in
which each picture had a special meaning for us.

Another priority after the war was the development of the garden. The first Lady Heathcoat
Amory was of Scottish descent, a keen gardener
in the tradition of her country. The development
took the form of a large kitchen garden full of
flower borders a little distance from the main
garden. In front of the house were broad and formal terraces, ornate with bedding-out. We began
to make alterations bit by bit to soften this effect,
and to give place to more and more of the new and
exciting plants brought into the country by the
collectors of this century. The empty bowling
green with its grand yew hedges was converted
to the water garden with statues and stone seats.

However, the idea of a 'Garden in the Wood'
became our chief ambition. My husband, always a
collector by nature, became particularly fascinated
by plants. For my part, I especially enjoyed the
planning of open spaces and vistas in the thick wild
wood which we had cleared, as well as arranging
plants, shrubs and trees in appropriate surround-
ings. The result of these combined efforts, with the
helping hands of many others, is the garden of
today, containing a wide range of horticulture
from the smallest to the largest blooms.

It is a joy, for me especially, and for others of
the Heathcoat Amory family, that Knightshayes
is now in the capable and devoted hands of the
National Trust, and that it will continue to be
filled with visitors, who will feel, it is hoped, the
warmth, welcome and happiness that have ani-
mated it in the past.

KNIGHTSHAYES COURT

Knightshayes Court is one of several hundred large country houses built by the Victorians in the boom years of agricultural and industrial development during the 1860s and early 1870s. It was the home of the Heathcoat Amory family, whose fortune was first established by John Heathcoat, a pioneer in the manufacture of lace and a textile entrepreneur, first in Nottingham and then Tiverton. He died in 1861, leaving his grandson, Sir John Heathcoat Amory, to consolidate the family's position near Tiverton by building Knightshayes, a house that befitted the owner of what was by then the largest lace-making enterprise in the world.

Architects of Victorian country houses tended to be specialists, often designing dozens of houses in the course of their careers. Knightshayes, however, was exceptional because its architect, William Burges (1827–81), was primarily a builder of churches and a decorator. At the age of fourteen Burges had fallen in love with thirteenth-century

Sir John Heathcoat Amory   *William Burges*

Gothic architecture, which became his life-long obsession. During his comparatively short career, some of the most bizarre interiors ever conceived during the nineteenth century were the product of his fertile imagination. Building at Knightshayes began in 1869, and by 1874 the house was structurally complete, but by then architect and client were at odds over the interior decoration. Burges had presented his ambitious plans in a handsome folio album, but these were far too lavish for Sir John's taste, and someone more conventional, John Dibblee Crace (1838–1919), was commissioned to complete the work, which he achieved by 1883. Even so, Sir John was uneasy about the brightly painted rooms, and much of Crace's work was later covered up.

Knightshayes remained the Heathcoat Amorys' family home until the second Sir John's death in 1972, when he generously gave the house to the National Trust. Since then, the Trust has endeavoured to maintain the exceptional woodland garden created by the Heathcoat Amorys and to restore the house to its nineteenth-century state.

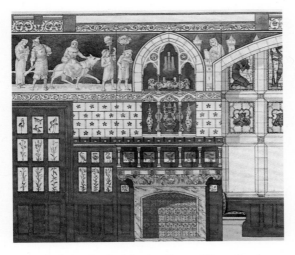

Burges's design for the Morning Room. His medieval vision of Knightshayes was only partly realised

(Right) Rosa banksiae 'Lutea' on the outside of the house

TOUR OF THE HOUSE

THE APPROACH

Knightshayes is approached past gate-piers and a lodge designed by William Burges in 1871. Early plans of the former incorporated a small roofed bridge, as over a lychgate, but this was never built and now the gates themselves have gone. The drive curves uphill, following the course of its predecessor to a Georgian house which stood just south of the present building. No trace of it remains, but several vast trees shading the drive date from that era. Among them is a Turkey oak some 50 metres high, reputedly the largest of its kind in the country.

The Exterior

THE SOUTH FRONT

To the right of the drive appears a terraced garden and above it Knightshayes, built of red Hensley stone with Ham stone dressings. Compared to Burges's contemporary work at Cardiff Castle, it seems restrained, being accurately described by the *Building News* in 1870 as 'stately and bold and its medievalism is not obtrusive'. Victorian connoisseurs would have admired the 'muscular' Gothic elevation of the façade, the unmoulded mullions,

The entrance front

The south front

and windows only occasionally punctuated with plate tracery quatrefoils. At first sight only a slight asymmetry and the addition of a corner oriel window suggest Burges's waywardness, but closer inspection of detail reveals his authorship: massive gargoyles and stylised leaves and an angel figure in the centre gable demonstrate his enthusiasm for thirteenth-century French architecture. East of this main block is a smaller gabled service wing, tucked well away, as the Victorians preferred. The conservatory to the west was added in 1963.

THE ENTRANCE FRONT

The drive skirts the north-west corner of the house and passes the single-storey Smoking Room annexe designed by Ernest George in 1902. An early watercolour sketch (illustrated on p. 1) shows that Burges planned an immense staircase tower to rise from this corner, but only the crenellated stump was built. Turning its corner, you reach the entrance front, where the windows are larger, lighting the Great Hall within. High up on a small belfry sits a stone talbot, or hound (from the crest of the family's coat of arms illustrated on the inside back cover), guarding the approach. Projecting at right angles to the main body of the house is the Billiard Room, wittily decorated by Burges with a frieze of billiard balls. Beyond is a small service court (not open to visitors), where Burges at one time considered placing a medieval-style kitchen with a tall conical roof, as at Glastonbury Abbey – an idea that was unfortunately abandoned.

The Interior

THE PORCH

The house is entered through the north porch beneath a hooded medieval figure acting as a lantern-bearer over the door. Carved in the arch are the words:

God by whose gift this worke I did begin
Conserve this same from skaith [damage] from
    shame from sin
Lord as this building built was by thy Grace
Mak it remain still with the builders' race.

The sculptor was Thomas Nicholls, who worked on many of William Burges's buildings, but the origin of the verse remains a mystery and, unhappily, 'skaith' occurred all too often in the following hundred years.

THE GREAT HALL

It was no surprise that Burges, as a Gothic Revival architect, chose to create an extravagant imitation of a medieval vaulted hall, but there the similarity ends, for the Hall was normally used by the family only for afternoon tea.

THE BURGES DESIGN

As in any great medieval house, the Hall is preceded by a screens passage, although in this case built of teak and partly glazed, above which is a gallery. The gallery parapet is pierced with openings sup-

The Great Hall in the nineteenth century

(Right) Burges's design for the Great Hall fireplace

porting four coloured and gilded shields, the first of many heraldic devices for which the Heathcoat Amorys had a passion.

The walls and roof of the Hall were to be elaborately stencilled and the whole room lit by windows containing heraldic glass. Against the south wall was to be a massive teak chimneypiece rising into the curve of the roof space. This had a crenellated mantelpiece pierced by more openings, each one filled with a gorgeous ceramic vase. The fireplace itself was to be built of grey marble backed with coloured tiles illustrating Aesop's fable of Reynard the Fox.

The roof trusses spring from corbels, which were carved as 'heads representing the conditions of Life'. On the south wall these comprise four figures: a cowled lady spinning, a harvester in hat and smock carrying sheaves of corn and a sickle, a scholar reading, and a soldier in chain-mail bearing a crossbow. From under the gallery a lady leans forward holding a flower. From the north wall

One of Burges's carved corbels in the Great Hall

peer a stone mason with his mallet, a bearded merchant with a bag of gold, a mitred bishop carrying a crozier, and, in the bay window, a chained prisoner supports two crowned figures, and another soldier wields a sword. Beneath the stairs is a more bizarre group of smaller corbels, representing fish, ducks, a chick emerging from its shell, a fox, a corpulent frog, a pair of clerics, a monkey and a tortoiseshell cat.

AFTER BURGES

Judging by a single surviving old photograph of the Hall, the main architectural features were built, but, like so much else in the house, it suffered several revisions and subsequent alterations. No stained glass was fitted and the stencilled decoration was simplified by J. D. Crace. In about 1914, the screen was demolished, the fireplace hood reduced in size and the stencilling erased.

RESTORATION

Fortunately, a combination of Burges's original designs, traces of coloured paintwork and some timber fragments removed to storage have allowed considerable restoration to be carried out in recent years. The stencilled roof is complete once more, the wall decoration is restored and, particularly satisfying, the teak screen is back to reimpose the original proportions on the room.

FURNITURE

RIGHT OF FIREPLACE:

The Melbury Road bookcase. In addition to his unusual architectural sculpture, Burges intended to furnish the house with his own brand of chunky and highly painted furniture. None was ever made for Knightshayes, but what might have been is demonstrated by the huge bookcase designed by Burges for his own London home in about 1860 and lent by the Ashmolean Museum in Oxford to the National Trust. It stands nearly four metres high and is remarkable for the painted scenes covering its front and sides. They portray Christian art on the left-hand side and pagan art on the right. The artists include Edward Burne-Jones, E. J. Poynter, Simeon Solomon, Albert Moore, Rossetti and H. Stacy Marks.

The high-backed marquetry chairs are early eighteenth-century Dutch and the central refectory table is seventeenth-century in style.

The pair of Victorian brass gasoliers were bought by the Trust and have been converted to electricity.

The Great Hall

Three trophies of the first Sir John Heathcoat Amory's stag-hunting exploits are exhibited on the walls.

PICTURES

HENRY STACY MARKS (1829–98)
Welcome

WILLIAM DE MORGAN (1839–1917)
An Eagle in a Tree, with Doves
De Morgan was the leading English pottery designer of the later nineteenth century. This design is for two ceramic tiles.

WILLIAM BURGES (1827–81)
The Hall Fireplace
This pen-and-ink sketch shows the architect's original design for the fireplace in this room.

AXEL HAIG (1835–1921)
The Winter Smoking Room, Cardiff Castle, 1870
Burges created this extraordinary vision of the Middle Ages for the immensely wealthy 3rd Marquess of Bute. If he had had his way, Knightshayes would have looked very similar.

SCULPTURE

SIR JACOB EPSTEIN (1880–1959)
Deirdre
This bronze is one of three studies Sir Jacob modelled on a young friend, Kathleen Balfour, in 1941.

TEXTILES

The four needlework pictures are by Herbert Newton Wethered, father of Joyce, Lady Heathcoat Amory. There are several other needlework pictures and chair seats to be seen around the house that are his work.

Pass through the Staircase Hall to the Smoking Room.

THE SMOKING ROOM

At Cardiff Castle, special tower rooms were set aside by Burges for use as winter and summer smoking-rooms; perhaps he intended something similar in the great tower he originally planned at the north-east corner of Knightshayes. It was never built, and Sir John Heathcoat Amory adopted the small Gentleman's Room next to the Billiard Room for the purpose. However, lack of a good smoking-room was obviously tiresome, for in 1901 the architectural firm of Ernest George & Yates was employed to provide 'an apartment specially dedicated to the use of tobacco', complete with lavatory and washroom.

The room was traditionally used for smoking after dinner and by younger members of the family during the day. Occasionally teas were served here, when the garden was open to the public or for meetings of the Tiverton Girl Guides.

With the exception of a new door pierced through to the entrance front, the panelled room remains unchanged. Until 1988 it was used as a shop by the National Trust, but has now been furnished again as if an Edwardian smoking-room, where visitors can rest.

FURNITURE

The moquette-covered chairs are comfortable rather than grand, and contemporary with the room. In the window bay is a *gramophone* dating from about 1930, which still plays 78 rpm records. To its right is an elaborate *longcase clock*. This was made as recently as 1975 by Mr Hoffman of London, but despite its youth reflects Edwardian taste for exotic woods and Baroque style. The same may be said of the *glazed bookcase* opposite, which was made by Harland & Wolff cabinetmakers as a copy of one that furnished the captain's cabin in a White Star liner during the 1900s. Carved and inlaid oriental pieces complete the ensemble.

The collection of miniature elephants was the gift of Mr Arthur Garnett.

PICTURES

After CLAUDE LORRAINE (1600–82)
Apollo and the Cumaean Sibyl
Apollo tried to seduce this Sibyl by promising to let her live as many years as there were grains of sand in her hand. She refused him, and he condemned her to live as a miserable old woman. The original is in the Hermitage in St Petersburg.

The Smoking Room

(Right)
The heraldic talbots on the staircase are taken from the family's crest

THE STAIRCASE

THE BURGES DESIGN

The monumental staircase is by Burges and is built of teak, as is the wall panelling to the height of the landing. A particularly whimsical feature were five carvings on the newel posts, each intended to illustrate an episode from the legend of St George and the dragon. Burges also planned a dazzling array of armorial stained glass for the lancet windows. The landing opens on to a small stone balcony overlooking the Hall. Burges added the intricately carved wooden screen in the doorway.

The inspiration was Islamic, a style much favoured by Burges, who considered it was 'allied in some respects, to that of the 13th century in Europe' and 'peculiarly adaptable ... in the decoration of the Gothic houses of the present day'.

AFTER BURGES

The first staircase casualty was the sequence of St George carvings. The Heathcoat Amorys preferred a heraldic scheme involving five generations of the family. Thus six heraldic talbots, each supporting an armorial shield, were carved by Harry Hems (1842–1916), a well-known Exeter sculptor. That

THE BEDROOM CORRIDOR

During one of the many redecoration campaigns in the house, this was replastered with a roughcast surface which absorbed light and made the corridor very dark. Investigations by the National Trust revealed a late nineteenth-century wallpaper beneath it, and, beneath that, J. D. Crace's original stencilled pattern. This had been applied by Campbell Smith & Co., a London firm of decorators happily still in existence, which, in 1976, was able to restore the walls to their original appearance.

THE BATHROOM AND DRESSING ROOM

These two rooms were designed by Burges, subsequently converted into a single bedroom and in 1937 reconverted for their present purposes. As a result, no part of the original decorative scheme

at the bottom of the stairs bears the arms of the first Sir John and his wife, Henrietta Unwin; at the top are those of Sir John's great-great-grandfather, John Amory, a Taunton grocer, and his wife, Anne Grove.

RESTORATION

In the 1970s, the National Trust restored the red-painted imitation mortar joints on the south wall according to Burges's original design. On the landing, although the Turkish screen had been removed in the 1950s, sufficient elements had been stored to allow for its replacement. This was the first restoration project undertaken by the Trust in a programme that has continued throughout the house ever since.

FURNITURE

On the quarter-landings are *two brass candelabra*, bought by the National Trust from St Mark's church, Dawlish (built 1849–50), shortly before its demolition in 1975. Above them hang the banners of a Knight of the Garter and the Order of St Michael and St George, awarded in 1968 and 1961 respectively to Derick, Viscount Amory, who was Chancellor of the Exchequer from 1958 to 1960.

The Bathroom

survived, so the rooms had to be re-equipped and furnished by the National Trust. Many of the fittings, dating from the turn of the nineteenth century, were brought from Lanhydrock in Cornwall. Burges's plans for Knightshayes indicate two bathrooms and four WCs on this floor of the main house.

THE BEDROOM

THE BURGES DESIGN

Burges's album of drawings shows the lower half of the walls painted yellow ochre, the upper as a frieze of birds, including ducks and pelicans amidst a red leaf pattern.

AFTER BURGES

If Crace produced designs for the Bedroom, they do not survive. His marble chimneypiece was moved to the east wing of the house in 1973, and a new chimneypiece carved from oak has been temporarily installed by the National Trust. The wallpaper and carpet date from 1979. The room is now noted more for its superb view of the park and distant view of the Heathcoat factory beyond.

FURNITURE

The mahogany four-poster bed is late eighteenth-century English, and the large wardrobe and corner cupboard are Dutch of the same period. All are indigenous to the house.

PICTURE

EVELYN DE MORGAN (1855–1919)
Moonbeams
Evelyn was the wife of the potter William de Morgan and niece of the painter Spencer Stanhope, who, together with the Pre-Raphaelite Burne-Jones, directly influenced her work. She adopted vaguely classical imagery for her complex allegories, which drew on a wide range of biblical and literary sources.

The opening between the Bedroom and Boudoir is new. Originally, the curved passage was a secluded alcove accessible only from the Boudoir.

THE BOUDOIR

THE BURGES DESIGN

Once again, Burges excelled himself in designing a room intended to evoke an essentially feminine retreat. The lower half of the wall was to be painted as if hung with embroidered fabrics beneath a wooden rail 'inlaid with little pieces of bevelled looking glass'. Above he planned a frieze illustrating scenes from Tennyson's *Dream of Fair Women* and a border of colourful birds. Over the chimneypiece swam a mermaid supporting a shelf to be piled high with art pottery. Stained glass would fill every window with images selected from Chaucer's *Legend of Good Women*. Finally, the ceiling would glitter with little circular mirrors dotted amongst low-relief medallions portraying subjects taken from Tennyson and Chaucer.

AFTER BURGES

None of this was achieved, although, as so often in Burges's work, he adopted his favourite motifs for use elsewhere. A Chaucerian Boudoir was built for Lady Bute at Cardiff Castle and a mermaid chimneypiece was installed in Burges's own Kensington home, Tower House. Meanwhile at Knightshayes, the Boudoir was conventionally treated by J. D. Crace with a marble fireplace and

Burges's design for the Boudoir ceiling. The present ceiling is based on a design by Crace

The Boudoir

cedar panelling. For the ceiling Crace chose a series of eight roundels painted with the signs of the Zodiac. Not long after completion they were obliterated.

RESTORATION

Crace's drawings, preserved in the Victoria & Albert Museum, were insufficiently detailed for the National Trust to make an accurate restoration. However, in 1981 the roundels were repainted by Ian Cairnie, closely following a similar scheme devised by Crace, which survives in a house at Hill Street, London. In 1991 the room was hung with wallpaper specially copied from a design by Burges, now at the RIBA. It is not known if this was ever previously manufactured.

FURNISHINGS

Unusual furnishings in the room include a nineteenth-century American treadle sewing-machine, a French musical box, a silver inkstand made by Elkingtons for the Great Exhibition of 1851, and a Tunbridgeware jewel box.

PICTURES

FRANK COPNALL (1870–1949)
Alexandra Seymour, Lady Heathcoat Amory
(1864–1942)
The wife of Sir Ian, the 2nd baronet, and mother of Sir John Heathcoat Amory, who gave Knights-hayes to the National Trust. She is said to be reading a letter sent by her son from school.

MINIATURE ON BUREAU:

LUCAS HENREY, 1898
Sir John Heathcoat Amory (1894–1972) as a child

ARTHUR DEVIS (1711/12–87)
*Mary Cawthorne, Mrs Morley Unwin (1724–96),
1750?*

The great-great-grandmother of the first Sir John's
wife, Henrietta, and a close friend of the poet
William Cowper, who wrote several of his poems
to her. He would have married her but for his concern over his mental stability, and she kept house
for him at Olney and Weston. Her son, William,
became Cowper's greatest confidant and drew him
into the Evangelical sect. This is the only early
family portrait at Knightshayes.

ENGLISH, eighteenth-century
Girl in a Red Dress
This portrait is painted on glass and is indigenous
to Knightshayes.

THE BURGES ROOM

The great album that Burges presented to the
Heathcoat Amorys in 1873 included a typically
ambitious design for this bedroom but as usual, his
plans were never realised. By the time the National
Trust acquired Knightshayes the room was painted
in a neutral cream colour and, apart from the fireplace, had no architectural features. It was
used as a staff bedroom until eventually vacated

Burges's design for this bedroom was never realised until redecorated by the National Trust in 2002

allowing the opportunity to redecorate the room as Burges intended. The upper walls are painted with birds perched on stylised branches and identified in gothic script. A similar avian theme was used by Burges at his Buckingham Street house in London. The fireplace is enclosed beneath a painted hood and the ceiling decorated with an enriched geometric pattern.

FURNISHINGS

These are on loan. They include the Golden Bed designed in 1879 for the architect's own guest bedroom at the Tower House in London, and a pair of painted cabinets also designed by Burges in 1858 for his patron Herbert Yatman. All three pieces are on loan from the Victoria and Albert Museum. The cabinet was designed by H & J Cooper and painted by Lewis Day. In 1878 it was exhibited at the Paris exhibition. It is known as the *Princess Cabinet* since the pictures and inscription are based on Tennyson's poem, The Princess. It is on loan from Mrs Jane Swire.

Burges designed the wallpaper in the lavatory

THE CORRIDOR

In planning a country house, a Victorian writer on the subject admitted it was 'difficult to select positions for convenience which shall at the same time be suitable for privacy. The principles of English delicacy are not easily satisfied'. It was therefore suggested that 'small ante lobbies are always useful'. The location of this water-closet fulfils these requirements admirably. The wallpaper is another example of a Burges copy, but taken from a manufactured design. It was hung in 1991.

FURNISHINGS

On the landing to the back stairs stands an oak buffet designed by the architect William White (1825–1900) for a contemporary Devon country house, Bishops Court, near Exeter. It was bought by the National Trust when the contents of that house were dispersed in 1994.

PICTURES

WILLIAM WIDGERY (1822–93)
Winter Landscape

Widgery was a prolific Devon born artist who lived for many years on Dartmoor.

RICHARD WESTALL RA (1766–1836)
Cardinal Bourchier, Archbishop of Canterbury, and Rotheram, Archbishop of York, endeavouring to persuade Elizabeth Grey, the Queen Dowager, to suffer her son, the Duke of York, to leave the sanctuary of Westminster Abbey, whither she had fled from the Duke of Gloucester, afterwards Richard III
Watercolour. Exh.RA, 1800.
Photograph of Sir Ian Heathcoat Amory.

TEXTILES

The textile needlework pictures, after part of the Sheldon Tapestry Map, and a *Mountain Landscape* by Jan I Brueghel, are by Herbert Wethered, father of Joyce, Lady Heathcoat Amory.

THE EXHIBITION ROOM

This was originally a bedroom which now accommodates changing exhibitions of material related to Knightshayes.

THE REAR LOBBY

This thoroughfare is reached at the bottom of the back stairs where it links the house to the former servants' quarters in the east wing. It also provided access to the male domain of the Billiard Room, which was separated, like its Smoking Room counterpart at the west end of the house, from the main reception rooms.

PICTURES

RUSSIAN, 1954
The Black Sea off Crimea
Presented to Viscount Amory by the Soviet leaders Marshal Bulganin and President Khrushchev during their visit to Britain in 1957. Lord Amory was then Minister of Agriculture in the Macmillan government.

BRITISH, 20th-century
Derick, Viscount Amory, KG (1899–1981)
A younger brother of Sir John Heathcoat Amory, 3rd Bt, who gave Knightshayes to the National Trust. Lord Amory was Chancellor of the Exchequer between 1958 and 1960, when he was created Viscount Amory of Tiverton.

CORNELIUS VARLEY (1781–1873)
Two drawings of Tiverton showing the church of St Peter above the River Exe and the Heathcoat factory. They are dated 1824 and were done with a mobile *camera obscura* that enabled images to be projected on to a table and then traced on paper.

WILLIAM BURGES (1827–81)
Architectural drawings
These are part of a large collection of drawings produced in the office of William Burges in the 1860s. Two are watercolour perspectives of the house as proposed, and the remainder are working drawings made during the design stage.

THE FAMILY ROOM

In the original plan for the house this room was labelled 'the Gentleman's Room', another name for a smoking-room, which was its purpose until the new one was built in 1901. More recently it became known as the Gun Room, but all the fittings and a fireplace on the east wall have now disappeared. In 1989 it was converted into a small exhibition room for family memorabilia and photographs.

THE BURGES DESIGN

Burges, as usual, drew up an elaborate scheme for decorating the room: a ceiling painted with the sun in its centre surrounded by signs of the Zodiac, the four winds and two figures that would 'personify the present and future'. The walls were divided, as now, by a picture rail, the upper half lined out and painted with figures in niches 'showing the occupations of the year', and below, painted red. The chimneypiece featured a stag hunt with the heads of hounds bursting from the canopy.

AFTER BURGES

As usual, Crace's scheme was less ambitious, but still too colourful for some and it was removed

This cup was made by Omar Ramsden to celebrate the many golf championships Lady Heathcoat Amory won

earlier this century. His painted ceiling has been restored by the National Trust and his wallpaper reproduced, copying the pattern from an original fragment found on a wall in the adjoining lavatory. Unusually, it is hung horizontally.

PICTURES AND FURNISHINGS

The room now houses a small exhibition of family memorabilia and other treasures, including a collection of apple green Worcester porcelain of the Dr Wall period, c.1770; the bust of Sir John Heathcoat Amory by Sir Jacob Epstein; and a delightful watercolour by W. P. Key, showing an outing by train from the Tiverton factory to Teignmouth in 1854. Photographs near the window show the house during the First World War, when the entire ground floor had been equipped as a military hospital accommodating 75 patients. Alexandra, Lady Amory herself took on a supervising role and is shown in one of the photographs. Another photograph shows the indoor tennis court 30 years later during the Second World War, when the house was used by convalescing American airmen.

THE GOLF ROOM

If Burges devised a decorative scheme for this room, it is not known. It was formerly described as the waiting room, probably for those with business to discuss with a member of the family. For some years it was used by the National Trust as a scullery, when the Billiard Room acted as a restaurant, but in 1989 it was converted into an exhibition room illustrating Joyce, Lady Heathcoat Amory's golfing career. As Joyce Wethered, she was four times winner of the British Ladies Open Golf Championship during the 1920s. Some of her many trophies are now displayed here. The large silver cup was made by Omar Ramsden (1873–1939), one of the foremost English silversmiths.

THE BILLIARD ROOM

THE BURGES DESIGN

As part of the male domain, every well-appointed Victorian country house had a separate billiard-room equipped with its own lavatory and wash-room tucked away in the corner. Knightshayes was no exception, and Burges gave much thought to its plan and decoration. After experimenting with designs for a bow-fronted room aligned parallel to the house, the present room was designed with ample top lighting from a large skylight (now covered in). For decoration Burges stipulated that the ceiling should be painted and gilded, 'with the addition of small silvered glasses' to represent stars on red and blue ground; the walls to have 'red lines on white ground with medallions containing figures of virtues and various animals representing the vices' above polished mahogany panelling. A marble fireplace with a gilded and mirrored overmantel was to have completed the ensemble.

AFTER BURGES

Although the medallion figures of the Virtues were probably never executed, the Vices are represented in seven carved animal corbels: the Seven Deadly Sins. Pride is a vulture-like eagle, Covetousness a goose with purse and scrolls, Lust a ram plucking a harp, Anger a growling wolf, Gluttony a plump sow, Envy a fox, and Sloth a sleepy animal with cobwebs on his back. In contrast, an eighth corbel depicts an owl, symbol of Wisdom. Burges's fireplace was never built, but the walls were repainted and the ceiling stencilled in 1999 following Crace's original scheme.

FURNITURE

Until 1988 the room was used by the National Trust as a restaurant. It is now a billiard-room once more, reunited with the original table, built by Thurston's of London. This probably dates from the early nineteenth century, since the base was formerly wooden, although it has now been converted to slate. The leather upholstered bench comes from Treberfydd House in Wales. The large sideboard is one of the few pieces of furniture in the house designed by Burges. It was made for

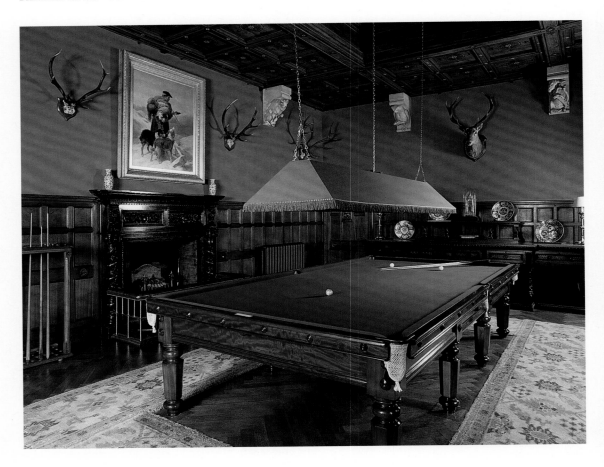

The Billiard Room

Worcester College, Oxford, where Burges was employed in 1874–9 to redesign the interior of James Wyatt's dining-hall. In 1975, some years after the Fellows of the College had decided to revert once more to an eighteenth-century interior, this major piece of furniture was loaned to Knightshayes.

PICTURES

RICHARD ANSDELL, RA (1815–85)
The Lost Sheep
Ansdell was the 'Raphael of Sheep', well known for his Highland scenes in the style of Landseer. Given to the National Trust by Miss Affleck of Sidmouth.

THOMAS BLINKS, RA (1860–1912)
Stag at Bay

THE DINING ROOM

THE BURGES DESIGN

In this room William Burges's ambitions again outstripped his clients'. He proposed that the walls should be entirely panelled in walnut with 'a shelf running all round for china' and above this, on each element of a frieze, a carved 'letter forming an inscription round the room'. The ceiling would be coloured and gilded and the stained glass would illustrate the fables of Aesop. As an additional luxury, the room would have a pair of painted and gilded chimneypieces with tall hooded canopies studded with armorial devices.

(Right) The Dining Room

AFTER BURGES

Of this decorative scheme, nothing apparently was executed save the carving on the doors and a reduced version of the panelling. The sculpted corbels, depicting animals, birds and human faces, lack Burges's unconventional style and may be by J. D. Crace. Certainly there are drawings of the ceiling by Crace in the Victoria & Albert Museum, which imply that he adapted the decoration from Burges's designs. But Crace's work too has suffered badly. At the end of the nineteenth century his ceiling, frieze and walls were covered in lincrusta paper to simulate plaster, and during the 1950s the room was again altered, when a kitchen complete with Aga was installed against the east wall and the room partitioned lengthways. Sir John maintained a workshop in the window bay.

RESTORATION

One of the National Trust's first tasks at Knights-hayes was the restoration of this room. With the aid of paint traces and the Crace drawings, Campbell Smith & Co. repainted the ceiling in

The breakfast table in the Dining Room

The over-mantels in the Dining Room were designed to display art pottery

black, white and red on the pine beams. Careful removal of the lincrusta paper revealed Crace's frieze and inscription, almost undamaged, with quotations from Robert Burns: 'BE BLEST WITH HEALTH AND PEACE AND SWEET CONTENT; KEEP THY TONGUE AND KEEP THY FRIENDS; COME EASE, COME TRAVIL, COME PLEASUR, COME PAIN, MY WARST WORD IS WELCOME AND WELCOME AGAIN.' Crace had also papered the room but it proved impossible to save, and new paper copied from one of his designs for the House of Lords has replaced it. Two more maxims, in Latin, occur in Crace's version of the two chimneypieces. They read 'CALET FOCUS CALET COR' ('A warm hearth makes the heart warm') and 'NE FOCIAS IGNEM GLADIO' ('Stir not the fire with the sword').

The National Trust has now arranged the room as if prepared for breakfast by using just the smaller table in the window bay and plate warmers on the sideboard. A vivid description of the sideboard in use during the early twentieth century was recorded by a guest, Miss March Phillips:

On a hunting day it was such fun staying at Knightshayes – the sideboard loaded with cold ham, galantine and other meats, sliced bread and a pile of greaseproof paper and you just went and made your own sandwiches and took as much as ever you wanted.

Reminiscing on family life at that time, Lord Amory recalled how his grandmother, Lady Henrietta, would organise entertainments for everyone over lunch: popular pastimes were hunting, driving or shooting in the winter, cricket or croquet in the summer. On more formal occasions the large dining-table was laid with the family silver, brought up from the basement safe. It could seat up to 30 diners, who were waited upon by the butler and footmen.

FURNISHINGS

The set of fifteen mid-nineteenth-century dining-chairs was bought by the National Trust from Llanyblodwel in Shropshire where they were once owned by John Parker, rector of that parish from 1845 to 1860.

The converted gasolier matches those hanging in the Great Hall and was bought by the Trust in 1976.

PICTURES

FROM THE LEFT OF THE DOOR:

ELEANOR FORTESCUE BRICKDALE (1871–1945)
St. Benezet of Avignon

FREDERIC CAYLEY ROBINSON (1862–1927)
Evening Idyll

HENRY STOCK (1853–1930)
Fire and Sea

E. BLAIR LEIGHTON (1853–1922)
Tristram and Isolde

BRITISH, nineteenth-century
Horseman

Man with a scythe

ARTHUR HUGHES (1832–1915)
The Forest of Arden

EDWARD BREWTNALL (1846–1902)
The Three Ravens

ELEANOR FORTESCUE BRICKDALE (1871–1945)
Some have entertained Angels Unaware

CERAMICS

The pots are in the style of the decorative lustreware produced for display in the late nineteenth century.

THE MORNING ROOM

THE BURGES DESIGN

In Burges's early drawings this room is shown with a conventional square plan, but he soon altered this to the present octagon and for decoration devised a luxurious combination of materials and colours. On the floor he wanted carpets of 'Turkish, Persian, Indian and other Eastern production'. The walls would be partially panelled in ebonised wood framing tiles painted with flowers and birds. Above this, a frieze would circle the room painted with grisaille figures on a blue ground 'illustrating the Heroes and Heroines of the Fairytales'. A similar scenario filled the stained glass. Against the north wall there was to be a Gothic chimneypiece in red 'Emperor Marble', and in the four corner recesses were carved and gilded shelves, supported by brass columns for the display of 'objects of art'. Finally, the ceiling

Madonna and Child with St Jerome and St Sebastian; by Matteo di Giovanni (Morning Room)

would be panelled in divisions painted blue and red and decorated with swirling arabesques and fancifully exotic birds.

AFTER BURGES

The principal architectural elements of the room and doors carved with family monograms are the only survivors of Burges's extraordinary proposal. Crace's scheme, including the ceiling, for which a drawing survives on paper watermarked 1874, was presumably executed, but in the course of the twentieth century this too was eradicated. In the 1950s the room was adapted into a dining-room with French windows pierced through to the garden. Walls and a new false ceiling were painted white.

RESTORATION

In 1975 the National Trust began restoring the room. Crace's original compartmented ceiling was revealed and repainted using a dark brown ground with a new centrepiece and motto 'HEALTH LONG LIFE WEALTH HAPPINESS'. Heraldic shields on the corbels refer to various generations of the Heath-coat Amory family. The walls are hung with a red velvet fabric, following the recent discovery of red threads in a corner of the window bay and an early twentieth century inventory description of the room. The wooden chimneypiece is a replace-ment by the National Trust, as is the carpet, which was specially woven to incorporate the family's talbot crest.

FURNISHINGS

Two recent Victorian additions to the room are the octagonal oak centre-table, possibly designed by A. W. N. Pugin (1812–52) for the Houses of Parliament, and the glittering brass chandelier bought in Plymouth in 1970. The spinet is by the London firm of Longman & Broderick. It is dated 1778 and was recently restored to a playable condition.

CERAMICS

In the four alcoves is an exceptional collection of seventeenth-century maiolica formed after the last war by Sir John Heathcoat Amory.

PICTURES

EITHER SIDE OF THE DOOR TO THE CORRIDOR

After REMBRANDT (1606–69)
Self-portrait
A copy of a picture in the Rijksmuseum in Amsterdam.

Attributed to GIOVANNI BOLTRAFFIO
(c.1466–1516)
St John the Baptist

FIREPLACE WALL

Manner of ROGIER VAN DER WEYDEN
(c.1400–60)
The Annunciation
Panel
Possibly part of an altarpiece from a convent in Segovia.

The Library

Matteo di Giovanni (1435–95)
Madonna and Child with St Jerome and St Sebastian
St Jerome (on the left) holds a stone, recalling his penitence as a hermit in the Syrian desert. St Sebastian was a Roman soldier transfixed with arrows for his Christian faith.

Attributed to Giulio Romano (c.1499–1546)
Detail from a cartoon

Manner of Holbein (1497–1543)
Lady with a white cap

Workshop of Lucas Cranach the Elder (1472–1553)
The Nativity

Sebastiano Ricci (1659–1734)
Christ healing the lame man

Crossing the Hall Corridor, you pass the garden door on your left. The panels resplendent with family heraldry above the door were designed by Crace and are now the only stained glass in the house. Ahead is the Library.

THE LIBRARY

A library was an essential component in every Victorian gentleman's country house. Samuel Amory formed the nucleus of this collection.

THE BURGES DESIGN

Burges seized his opportunity for another extraordinary room. He aimed to integrate red-stained oak Gothic bookcases with niches containing exotic pottery and an embossed leather frieze gilded and painted with portraits of classical authors. In the centre of the north wall he envisaged a massive castellated and gabled chimneypiece encompassing 'A lady holding the Amory shield and crest and above statues of four great authors'. The ceiling introduced one of Burges's favourite motifs: the gilded mini-vault like a jelly-mould, an idea he borrowed from Arabic architecture.

27

Burges's design for the Library

AFTER BURGES

In fact it was Crace who, once again, tempered this design with a milder version of his own. He installed Gothic bookcases with linenfold panelling and shelves to display pottery. Once again, twentieth-century alterations have made their mark. In the 1950s the bookcases were cut down and shorn of their Gothic embellishments, the chimneypiece was replaced and the ceiling lowered. A late nineteenth-century photograph of the room, however, showed that elaborately carved corbels and the 'jelly-mould' vaults had been built, and in 1984 the National Trust began restoring the room.

RESTORATION

When the false ceiling was removed, the Trust discovered a pair of copper armorial roundels, but also that the corbels had been hacked off during the previous ceiling alterations. Happily, Crace's fireplace and a few fragmentary details of the shelves had been stored so that with the additional evidence of a Crace drawing showing the west wall and two early photographs, a complete restoration of the walnut fittings was possible in 1998.

FURNISHINGS

The old photographs show the room in use as a family sitting-room, and it has been furnished as such by the National Trust. The Louis XIV-style Boulle bracket clock was given to Sir Ian Heathcoat Amory in 1910 on his retirement as Master of the Tiverton Staghounds, the hunt he founded in 1896.

The chandelier was bought by the National Trust from a church in Worcestershire.

PICTURES

ENGLISH, nineteenth-century
John Heathcoat (1783–1861)
The founder of the family textile business.

BRITISH, 1885
Ludovic Heathcoat Amory (1881–1918)
Ludovic was the youngest son of Sir John, the builder of Knightshayes and was killed in the First World War. He married in 1911 and had three sons, two of whom were killed in the Second World War.

BRITISH, nineteenth century
Samuel Amory (1784–1857)

THE DRAWING ROOM

Writing in 1864 on country-house planning, Robert Kerr considered, 'It is in this particular apartment, if in no other, that the designer may venture to take a little licence'. Certainly at Knightshayes the Drawing Room would have witnessed the climax of Burges's ingenuities as a decorator.

THE BURGES DESIGN

For his theme, Burges selected chivalry, which befitted a room always regarded as 'the lady's apartment essentially', assigning the north wall chimneypiece to play a major role by featuring *The Assault on the Castle of Love*. In the album Burges explained its construction: the 'lower portion of marble and the upper part of sculpted stone coloured and gilded'. He intended the completed structure to resemble a medieval castle. Painted across the mantelpiece were knights, who had fallen during the assault, tended by their squires, whilst from the battlements peeped the crowned and wimpled faces of their female quarry. Above them a painted frieze depicted 'figures showing the various conditions of life, offering their hearts to Cupid'. To add realism to the idea, Burges designed a columned gallery behind the mantelpiece, accessible from a secret spiral staircase, allowing Victorian ladies to join their painted counterparts and wave at the gentlemen below!

AFTER BURGES

Only the staircase and a blander version of the mantelpiece were built. The fireplace itself, the green wall-panelling (which was enriched with paintings of birds and flowers set with mother-of-pearl), the frieze illustrated with 'paintings in oil of various love stories', the stained glass, the star-spangled ceiling and a second great chimneypiece on the east wall, carved with 'Heraldry and above, statues of Writers upon Love', were not.

Predictably, it was all too much for the Heathcoat Amorys, and it was Crace's chimneypiece of walnut, alabaster, red Devon marble, mirror glass and de Morgan tiles that eventually filled the north wall. This in its turn was removed in 1946 and an eighteenth-century-style replacement

Burges's design for the Drawing Room

installed when the house was gradually Georgianised. Finally in 1963 the west bay was enlarged by the removal of a central marble column from the twin-arched opening and a long horizontal beam was substituted.

RESTORATION

By 1980 there seemed to be no nineteenth-century components left in the room, but suspicions remained that a false ceiling had at one time been installed and these were confirmed by the simultaneous rediscovery of Burges's working drawings. Plaster ceiling panels, dated 1889 on the back, were removed to reveal a brightly coloured design related to Burges's original album drawings and featuring the gilded 'jelly-mould' concavities of which he was so fond. At the same time traces of blue, red and gold stencilled paintwork were found beneath several layers of cream paint on the window mullions, and these have been restored.

Pencilled on one of the mullions is the date 1883, when presumably the earlier alteration began. The work of restoration was carried out in 1981 by Stansells, a Taunton firm.

Having restored so much of the room's nineteenth-century decoration, the National Trust was able to complement it with a marble chimneypiece designed by Burges and carved by an Italian, Fucigna, for the hall at Worcester College, Oxford in 1876. This massive structure – the mantelpiece alone weighs one and a half tons – had been removed from its original site in 1966, when an eighteenth-century scheme was restored to the hall in preference to Burges's later embellishments. The college generously gave the chimneypiece to the Trust and it now stands in the Drawing Room in the same scale and position planned by the architect for his original extraordinary essay on chivalry. The coat of arms is that of Sir Thomas Cookes, founder of the college. Finally, in 1982, the west bay column and arches were restored, but in timber painted to match the stone originals.

The cabinet in the Drawing Room was designed by H. W. Batley and made by Henry Ogden & Son around 1878

River Scene in Picardy; by Richard Parkes Bonington (Drawing Room)

The Drawing Room

FURNISHINGS

The National Trust hopes that Victorian furniture will gradually be acquired to fill the room as it deserves. The 1899 inventory lists a staggering total of six settees, seventeen tables, twelve armchairs, and ten other chairs amongst its contents, much of which had to be moved when the family entertained. The room witnessed its first ball in 1872 (see p. 47) and thereafter annual servants' balls were held here, when traditionally the butler formally invited the lady of the house to take the floor for the first dance.

The most impressive piece now in the room is the large cabinet against the east wall purchased by the Trust. This was designed by H. W. Batley and made by Henry Ogden & Son of Manchester. It is almost identical to another Batley cabinet exhibited at the Paris International Exhibition of 1878. Most of the pots now displayed on it were made in Devon potteries around the turn of the century. They are on loan from the Royal Albert Memorial Museum, Exeter.

The three tables are also interesting, all bought in recent years by the National Trust. The large central table was designed in 1828 by Anthony Salvin for Mamhead House near Dawlish, as were the pair of standard lamps. All are made of light oak taken from the Mamhead estate. The table to the left of the column was made specially by Burges for Cardiff Castle. It was intended to accommodate a palm to sprout leaves through the hole in its centre. The table to the right is a mid-nineteenth-century library-table by Gillow's of Lancaster. The Turkey carpet comes from Wembury House, Devon.

PICTURES

These are the remaining nucleus of the picture collection Sir John and Lady Heathcoat Amory put together after the Second World War. They gave four of its major treasures to other institutions: Lancret's *La tasse de chocolat* and Van Goyen's *An Estuary with Fishing Boats* to the National Gallery; the *Mystic Marriage of St Catherine* (generally attributed to Poussin) to the National Gallery of Scotland; and the *Nativity* now attributed to the Master of the Prado Annunciation to the Birmingham City Art Gallery. A *Landscape* attributed to

Rubens was sold to provide an endowment for the house.

In the classic English way, the pictures were chosen to be lived with, not isolated in a picture gallery. The Heathcoat Amorys bought all their pictures through Agnew's, whose managing director, Sir Geoffrey Agnew, became a personal friend. According to Richard Kingzett, 'The private collection whose formation gave him the greatest pleasure was made by Sir John and Lady Heathcoat Amory'. It is therefore profoundly disappointing that so many of the Heathcoat-Amorys' cherished pictures should not have stood up to critical scrutiny since.

CLOCKWISE FROM LIBRARY DOORS:

JOHN GRAY (*fl.*1900–10)
Alexandra, Lady Heathcoat Amory, wife of Sir Ian Heathcoat Amory, 2nd Bt
Painted in 1906.

JOHN GRAY (*fl.*1900–10)
Sir John Heathcoat Amory, 1st Bt
Painted in 1907.

ENGLISH SCHOOL, twentieth-century
Sir Ian Heathcoat Amory, 2nd Bt

MARY EASTMAN (*fl.*1950s)
Sir John Heathcoat Amory, 3rd Bt

Attributed to JOHN CONSTABLE (1776–1837)
Poppies
Constable painted a few flower-pictures, but they differ in character from this.

Attributed to JOHN CONSTABLE (1776–1837)
Field Flowers and Berries in a Brown Pot
Constable painted a few flower-pictures, but they differ in character from this.

After J. M. W. TURNER (1775–1851)
The 'Sun of Venice' going to Sea
A copy of the picture Turner exhibited at the Royal Academy in 1843 (now in the Tate Gallery).

MARY EASTMAN (*fl.*1950s)
Joyce, Lady Heathcote Amory, wife of Sir John Heathcoat Amory, 3rd Bt

You leave the house through the Conservatory.

The Stables

THE CONSERVATORY

The Conservatory is one of the most recent additions to the garden, built in 1963 for growing tender, free-flowering plants throughout the year and for winter gardening. By 2004 the building's condition had deteriorated badly, despite years of continual maintenance. A major restoration programme is planned for 2005, following which the planting will reflect the Amory's interest in orchids and rhododendrons.

Turn left to walk along the terraces into the garden, or right to visit the Stables.

THE STABLES

North of the house is one more Burges building, the Stables. It is peculiarly Burgesian, with a Gothic asymmetric façade and dormer windows painted red. Now that it is surrounded on three sides by trees and partially creeper-covered, it appears, appropriately, mysteriously medieval. In the tradition of stables the building has four wings built around a courtyard of granite sets and dominated by a clock-tower. It comprised loose-boxes (now the restaurant and shop), a chaff house (now part of the shop), a hayloft (above the lavatories), more stabling (the lavatories), a cleaning and a harness room (now the reception area and exhibition room) and a carriage house (now the east restaurant).

Before the age of the motor car Sir Ian maintained three carriages: a Victoria, a brougham and a trap. In 1904 he acquired his first car, an Arrol Johnson, which in 1906 he succeeded in driving to Glasgow over a period of five days. Later he owned a Chrysler, then a Sunbeam and finally a series of Bentleys. Sir John's first car was a Stutz, while his brother Derick drove a more modest Austin Six.

As the family was always keen on hunting, the stables remained busy until the 1940s, when they were converted into living accommodation for convalescing airmen from the US Air Force. After the war they were used for two flats and storing garden machinery until 1988 when they were converted to provide the present visitor facilities.

33

THE GARDEN

Knightshayes garden is well-known, but the changes it has undergone since the 1870s, when it was first laid out, are as fundamental as any that occurred in the house. The original designer was Edward Kemp (1817–91), an eminent landscape gardener who began his career as a pupil of Paxton at Chatsworth and with Paxton was responsible for designing one of the most celebrated of Victorian parks at Birkenhead, in 1843–7. This was the first municipal park to be provided at public expense and it influenced the design of many others including Olmsted's Central Park in New York. Kemp was appointed Park Superintendent of Birkenhead, a position he held for 40 years, but this did not prevent him from accepting private commissions, which increased following the pub-lication of his book *How to lay out a Garden: A General Guide in choosing, forming or improving an Estate*

(1850). From this, one discovers that Kemp was a follower of Repton and the Picturesque tradition. He described his own preferred style as 'mixed':

Serpentine or wavy lines may be regarded as the characteristic features of the mixed style. Its object is beauty of lines and general variety ... intricacy, every species of variety, indefiniteness, extension of apparent boundaries, polish and connection, and specially its own traits.

It was Kemp who first trained 'luxuriant' creepers on the house, who constructed three terraces with formal bedding below the south front on the site of the kitchen garden of the old house, and who planted the yew hedges east of the house enclosing a bowling green. In his book he wrote, 'In the present artificial state of society, with every species of business conducted in an anxious and hurried manner ... a bowling green, as

The woods above the Pool Garden in spring

The mixed-shrub herbaceous borders beside the house

an appendage to a garden ... affords one of the least violent as well as the most domestic means of obtaining the desired relaxation in the open air.'

West of the house Kemp took advantage of a little valley to create a series of ponds, waterfalls and rockeries planted up in the American style including rhododendrons, kalmias, azaleas and conifers. He also planned the layout within the stepped and turreted walls of the large kitchen garden. This was split into triangular sections by paths and planted with yew and mulberry trees. A series of greenhouses accommodated vines, palms, melons, peaches and numerous exotic flower species including 'probably the finest example of *Alocasia thibautiana* in the country' and 'an unrivalled collection' of azaleas. The planting was carried out by the foremost nurserymen of the time, Veitch's of Exeter.

By the 1930s this Victorian scheme had become outmoded, not least because it relied so heavily on labour-intensive bedding-out programmes to create the annual splash of colour. (In the 1890s coleus was a favourite plant and there were 500 boxes of chrysanthemums alone along the south front.) The only significant addition to the garden had been the Fox and Hounds topiary on top of

yew hedges east of the house, which were cut in the 1920s, but that aside, the garden had declined into a mouldering token of its colourful past. 'In 1937', commented Lady Heathcoat Amory, 'the scope of the garden was confined to a few formal terraces, some bedding out, a tortuously clipped yew topiary and a small paved area with rose beds. The rest was given over to a bowling green and a large expanse of lawn.' Courageously, the Amorys decided to plan anew, even though both were beginners in the art of gardening. They wisely sought help and advice from a large number of friends and acquaintances including Lanning Roper, who helped redesign the Pool Garden, Graham Stuart Thomas, who offered advice over a number of years, Sir Eric Savill and Norman Hadden, who both added suggestions for the development of the Garden in the Wood and in the planting of tender shrubs, magnolias, rhododendrons, azaleas, herbaceous plants and bulbs.

Thus the garden as it now appears is a comparatively new creation. It has been described as embodying 'all that is best in modern gardening', no mean achievement, and attained only through the enthusiasm of Sir John and Lady Heathcoat Amory and their Head Gardener since 1963, Michael Hickson. Writing about his garden, Sir John, who in 1967 was awarded the Victoria Medal of Honour (the Royal Horticultural Society's highest honour), was unnecessarily modest: 'The game continues, never ending and never wholly satisfactory, pursuing a goal to which only time can lead one, and which is always round the corner. The old definition of gardening may be a good one: "Eleven months of hard work and one month of acute disappointment".' Neither did Lady Heathcoat Amory's interest in the garden flag, and in recognition of her work she too was awarded the VMH in 1981.

TOUR OF THE GARDEN

The garden divides into several distinct parts. Nearest the house are the Conservatory (see p. 33), the house borders and planting up the house walls. Below it are the Terraces, overlooking the park, and separated from it by a ha-ha and the South Garden. Immediately east of the house are three small formal gardens: the Paved Garden, the Pool Garden and the Fox and Hounds Topiary Garden. Beyond them rise the trees of the Garden in the Wood. West of the house and beyond the drive is the Azalea Dell. To the north-west is the Victorian kitchen garden, which borders the Douglas Fir Walk.

THE TERRACES

The Gardener's Chronicle in 1888 declared, 'The front and the sides of the house were beautifully covered to a considerable height'. Plants included *Magnolia grandiflora*, Banksian roses and honeysuckles. Today, where the house is stepped back to the service wing, there is a broad, mixed-shrub herbaceous border integrated with trefoil-shaped beds bounded by yew hedges planted in 1989.

The second terrace is now grassed over, save for the surviving topiary obelisks at the west end, which flank a lead cistern bought in 1950. They face a seat backed by Pfitzer Juniper at the east end. The stone urns and eagles had been added in the 1920s. Climbing the stairs is a wisteria which has survived from the kitchen garden of the old house.

The third terrace has a gravel path and a continuous border of tree peonies, roses and herbaceous plants in soft colours and silvers, adapted to the hot and dry conditions. It is linked on the east to a wide border of shrub roses and herbaceous plants in similar colours.

The lowest terrace retains the original paving pattern of the old rose garden, now grassed over but with the added attraction of the dolphin fountain in the centre. On the east side are crab apples,

and prominently, where once was the kitchen garden of the previous house, a vast Cedar of Lebanon framing the main prospect across the park. The view beyond is of the Heathcoat textile mill.

THE PAVED GARDEN

The gravel path on the top terrace leads eastwards to a group of yew-hedged enclosures. On the left is the Paved Garden, which is bisected by a path leading to a lead cistern dated 1727, which was bought from the Goldsmiths' Company. Either side are two stone benches that come from the Bank of England, lead figurines of the four seasons, and a pair of standard wisterias. The beds between the paving stones have been filled with alpines, small bulbs and plants chosen for their softly coloured silver and grey foliage, and pink, yellow and purple flowers. Next to the gravel path is a terraced border devoted to a mixture of small perennial alpine plants and bulbs.

THE POOL GARDEN

The adjoining battlemented, hedged enclosure was designed by Kemp as a bowling green, in which a round pond was excavated in 1957. It is planted with different species of waterlilies including the deep red 'Escarboucle', white *Nymphaea gladstoneana*, and the yellow 'Moorei', amongst which shubunkin (a variety of goldfish) and golden orfe swim. Reflected in the water is a Weeping Silver Pear tree and a Victorian sculpture of a bather. Behind the yew hedge is a superb *Acer pseudoplatanus* 'Brilliantissimum'.

THE FOX AND HOUNDS

South of the Pool Garden, hounds endlessly cavort after a fox, caught by the hedgeclipper's art. At the far end of their lawn there is a copy of the Borghese vase and, to its right, a gap in the hedge, through which those wishing to avoid the steps in

(Left) The Paved Garden
(Right) The Garden in the Wood

the Garden in the Wood may pass. Alternatively, on the other side of the hedge is a summer-house, and seats for those who prefer to admire the South Garden in comfort.

THE GARDEN IN THE WOOD

Creating the Garden in the Wood was a major enterprise during the 1950s and '60s, involving the removal of hundreds of trees. It now covers some ten acres bisected by the old church path which used to lead straight to Chevithorne church and

the family pew. The path is surrounded by shrubs underplanted with woodland herbaceous plants. The Heathcoat Amorys left several of the old Austrian and Scots Pines, oak and birch trees, amongst which were introduced a wide range of plants including peonies, hellebores and geraniums, as well as shrubs like magnolias, rhododendrons, cornus, buddleja and hypericum.

A large pine forms the centre of the first glade and around it the emphasis is mainly on camellias, magnolias, Japanese maples, rhododendrons and Kurume azaleas. Raised beds have been formed using peat blocks which have proved ideal for small plants and bulbs. To the east there are helle-bores, azaleas, acer, pieris, kalmia, other ericaceous shrubs and tree peonies, with rambling roses in the trees.

THE GLADE

By the end of the 1950s a new challenge presented itself with the Glade, which Sir John saw as 'just the place for lilies', sheltered to the south by a Mock Orange hedge planted at the end of the nineteenth century. A curving stone seat carved with griffins provides the focal point. To the west is the Flat Border for dwarf spreading rhododen-drons, *Enkianthus* camellias and creeping Canadian dogwood. North of the hedge is a wide border with a purple and blue, yellow and green colour scheme, created by euphorbia, hosta, meconopsis and other plants. The island bed is dominated by a pittosporum grouped in association with stachyurus, bergenia and tree peonies. The border behind the seat and the cedar summer-house has been planted to produce colours of a creamy-white and blue, and, finally, at the eastern end of the Glade is a tunnel-effect of variegated species of hydrangeas beneath the beech, pine and larch.

HOLLY'S WOOD

During the later 1960s this area of the garden finally reached its present size. To the north is an informal planting of trees and shrubs within the existing beech, oak, lime and larch. The plan-tation is known as Holly's Wood, named after

Herbert Hollinrake of Ottery St Mary, who was so generous with gifts of plants in the 1960s and '70s. Chinese rhododendrons and some Asiatic magnolias create a horseshoe planting effect on the northern fringe.

SIR JOHN'S WOOD

Sir John himself described the area as 'a larch wood, the trunks making an impressive back-ground with mysterious darkness beyond'. During the storm in January 1990 many trees were lost, and the darkness with them, but choicer plants survived, and the wood is now penetrated by two walks. The outer thrives with acer, photinia, osmanthus and herbaceous groups of actaea, tri-cyrtis, hosta, lilies and woodland gentians. The inner is similar, with large evergreens such as ilex, podocarpus, pieris, *Cupressus cashmeriana* with ground cover of ferns, mosses and dog-toothed violets. White foxgloves are also a special feature.

THE ARBORETUM

The Arboretum comprises a glade with oak trees and some conifers. The north side is bordered by conifers and grasses on this dry, south-facing bank. The south flank of ornamental trees – clethera, aralia and acer – is protected by a screen of oak and *Rhododendron ponticum*.

MICHAEL'S WOOD

The furthest south-east corner of the woods is named after the Head Gardener, Michael Hickson. Beneath the trees a wide range of plants has been established to provide contrasting foliage, shapes and colour all the year round. In particular there are prostrate dwarf conifers and swathes of hardy cyclamen – a particular favourite of Lady Amory.

THE SOUTH GARDEN

By 1954 it became clear that the large-leaved rhododendrons were not doing well in other parts of the garden, so this 3-acre tongue of land to the south was prepared for them where once had been a game covert and putting green. The woodland was thinned and interplanted with large exotic trees, including several varieties of *Nothofagus* (Southern Beech). But the glory of this garden is the rhododendrons, which provide sensational colour and scent in spring. Yet more colour is offered by interplanting of dogwoods and Japanese cherries protected by a thickly planted perimeter.

The Azalea Dell

THE AZALEA DELL

Still the Amorys had not finished. In 1970 they launched into one more major garden reclamation, the Azalea Dell, situated in the valley west of the house. In Kemp's day this area was known as the American Garden, and the valley contained an ambitious array of American and ericaceous plants, rockeries, ponds and waterfalls. Today only the land form, the pond and some old Mollis and Ghent azaleas betray the origins of a garden now reserved for a wide variety of shrubs and small trees and, in spring, rippling drifts of daffodils.

THE KITCHEN GARDEN

By now you will have noticed the walled Kitchen Garden, essential to any Victorian country house. It lies on a favourable slope of land between stepped walls and corner towers probably designed by William Burges although records of the garden are tantalisingly absent. The internal layout was, perhaps, by Edward Kemp and the garden's original importance can be judged from extensive descriptions in nineteenth-century gardening periodicals.

It remained in traditional use until the 1960s. In 2001 work started on recreating the plan of the old kitchen garden which has been planted taking advantage of new techniques and ideas, and is organically cultivated. The axial yew-hedged paths, the mulberry trees at the *rond-points* either side of the pond, and topiary at the south-west end are all original features. Produce from the garden is used in the stables restaurant and for sale to visitors.

THE DOUGLAS FIR WALK

In complete contrast to the rest of the garden is the stand of Douglas Fir in an area east of the kitchen garden. The species was introduced to Britain from the Rocky Mountains in 1827 and planted here as an avenue in the 1870s. Some trees have already reached about 45 metres and are among the largest in the country. This and other areas of the woodland park are more fully described in a separate Impey Walk leaflet.

THE HEATHCOAT AMORYS AND THEIR ARCHITECTS

JOHN HEATHCOAT

Knightshayes Court is the creation of two men of genius: the one made the industrial fortune that paid for the house, the other was an architect of extraordinary originality. The first was John Heathcoat, born into a Derbyshire farming family in 1783. His schooling was brief, to be followed by apprenticeship in the local hosiery trade where he soon demonstrated a precocious ability. By the age of 25 he had moved to Nottingham, bought up his master's business with a huge loan of £20,000 and designed and patented a machine that revolutionised the manufacture of lace. Until the building in 1808 of the 'Old Loughborough' (as

John Heathcoat, the founder of the family fortunes; by William Beetham (Rear Lobby)

Heathcoat's machine became known), lace was hand-made by the laborious 'pillow and bobbin' method. With the machine it could be produced in quantity far more quickly and cheaply. The invention bore fruit. By 1816 Heathcoat had moved with his wife and three children to Loughborough where he managed a factory housing 55 of the new machines.

His success had been meteoric, but on 28 June 1816 it came to an abrupt halt. That night the factory was attacked by a mob of drunken Luddites. Within half an hour Heathcoat's machines were smashed and his lace burnt by the wreckers, who mockingly described the demolition as 'a Waterloo job'. It was a devastating disaster, but Heathcoat's reaction was characteristically bold. Not wishing to risk further disruption to his business, he refused compensation of £10,000 offered by the county on condition that he rebuilt his factory in Loughborough, preferring instead to move to the safety of Devon, where he had already bought a mill. And so, followed by many of his loyal Loughborough workers, who walked the 200 miles, Heathcoat began anew in Tiverton.

It was an astute move. Tiverton's tradition of woollen goods manufacture could be traced back to the Middle Ages, using water power harnessed from the River Exe, but in 1816 the industry was declining and factories stood empty. Heathcoat flourished, expanding his interests into France and Sicily. In 1832 he was elected as Whig MP for Tiverton and represented the town continuously for the next 28 years.

The esteem in which Tivertonians held Heathcoat is summed up in a letter written in 1844 by one of his workers: 'We have all cause to pray for the life of Mr Heathcoat he is the best man that I ever knew in Tiverton for giving employment to the poor.' He was particularly interested in

A works outing to Teignmouth from the Heathcoat lace factory in August 1854; by W. P. Key (Family Room)

JOHN HEATHCOAT AMORY AND THE KNIGHTSHAYES ESTATE

education and would not employ anyone in his factory who could not read or write. The parents of children who worked for him were charged two pence per week whilst their children were being taught those subjects, and his daughter later opened a school for girls in what is now the Hartnoll Hotel. In 1841 he built the Heathcoat Schools next to the factory. One man who worked for him was Samuel Amory, a London lawyer and banker, who married his daughter Anne. Samuel's grandfather had moved from Taunton to London, where he became a well-known dissenting minister and where his father had worked as a banker in Clements Lane. John Heathcoat had no son, and so on his death in 1861, the Amorys' son John (the first to use the amalgamated surname Heathcoat Amory) was a natural choice to inherit the now well-established business. It provided employment for 1,100 workers and was to become by far the largest lace factory in the world.

Unlike his grandfather, John Heathcoat Amory was less interested in running the business than playing the role of country gentleman. In 1863 he married Henrietta Unwin, the daughter of a Colonial Office functionary, and he assigned the day-to-day running of the business to his brother-in-law's care. He was appointed Deputy Lieutenant of the county, Captain of the local volunteers and Justice of the Peace. Like his grandfather, he was elected Liberal MP for Tiverton, in 1869, but his political career was distinguished only by his support for the Interments Act of 1882. Until then a suicide's corpse was buried only between 9pm and 12 midnight within 24 hours of the verdict, usually by the police. As a humanitarian gesture, the Act allowed relatives of the deceased to bury the body at a reasonable hour. When Gladstone's government was defeated in 1874, Heathcoat Amory received a knighthood for 'political services' and he continued in Parliament until his resignation in 1885.

None of these public duties incurred very oner-
ous responsibilities and it left Heathcoat Amory
time to indulge his passion for shooting on his
Scottish estate in Perthshire, fishing at his lodge
in Norway, and especially hunting over Exmoor
with his three packs of hounds: stag hounds, fox
hounds and harriers. To accommodate his hunters
and to provide an appropriately grand house for his
family, he bought the Knightshayes estate.

The early history of the estate is vague. It is first
mentioned in the fourteenth century, when it was
occupied by a Robert de Knightenhaie. Then
follows a long gap in its history until the six-
teenth century when at least part of the estate was
owned by descendants of the Courtenay family,
Earls of Devon, whose seat had been at Tiverton
Castle. Towards the end of the seventeenth century, Knightshayes had passed to George Stucley,
a member of another prominent Devon family,
the Stucleys of Hartland Abbey and Affeton. On
several occasions he mortgaged the property as
security for considerable debts and for many years
Knightshayes was occupied by tenant farmers.

Meanwhile, Tiverton's wealth had shifted to a
new class of wool merchant as the textile trade
boomed. Several mercantile owners and tenants
are recorded at Knightshayes during the eighteenth
century until Ben Dickinson (1737–1806), the
wealthiest of Tiverton's merchant bankers, acquired the estate and built a new house in 1787.
It stood about 100 metres south of the present
mansion and apparently was painted white with a
south front 13.7 metres long. Today no trace or
image of it survives. In 1813 Ben Dickinson's
grandson, another Ben (1794–1857), inherited
the family's fortune and consolidated his position
by marrying Frances Walrond, sole heiress of
the nearby Bradfield estate. Ben took the name
Walrond and moved to his wife's home. On his
widow's death in 1866, efforts were made to sell
Knightshayes to John Heathcoat Amory, then living
at Bolham House nearby, but due to legal compli-
cations this took two years and 500 documents to
complete. Heathcoat Amory resolved to demolish
the existing Knightshayes and build afresh on the
site of the old kitchen garden, and at this point the
second genius in the story should be introduced.

*Sir John Heathcoat Amory, 1st Bt, the builder of
Knightshayes Court; by John Gray (Staircase)*

WILLIAM BURGES AND
KNIGHTSHAYES COURT

'Whatever looks best is best'

The man Heathcoat Amory chose for the job was
William Burges, described by Mark Girouard as
'one of the most Gothic of the Gothicists' among
nineteenth-century architects. As a young man
he had worked for another enthusiastic 'Goth',
Edward Blore, and travelled widely, even as far as
Constantinople, sketching feverishly as he went,
especially in France and Italy. At first his architectural commissions were few, but by the mid–1860s
he was at work on the three most important pro-
jects of his career: St Finn Barr Cathedral, Cork,
begun in 1862; the remodelling of Cardiff Castle
for Lord Bute, begun in 1865; and the designs

for the Strand Law Courts, published in 1867, although never built. Known as 'Billy' Burges, he was a familiar figure amongst the artistic avant-garde in London. He was a member of some half a dozen London clubs at any one time, a frequent lecturer on architectural subjects and an author of numerous works on antiquarian and architectural themes. His interests were varied but his allegiance to the medieval is emphasised again and again in all he did. 'I was brought up in the thirteenth-century belief and in that belief I intend to die', he proclaimed. He pursued this belief, not with slavish imitations, but in creating a fantastic Pre-Raphaelite dreamworld that encompassed not only the bare bones of architecture but also richly designed interiors filled with sculpture, stained glass, mosaics, furniture and metalwork. An addiction to opium no doubt fuelled his imagination, but his philosophy was simple: 'Rules are made only for incapables ... No rule can be deduced except the golden one *whatever looks best is best*'. He also said, 'Money is only a secondary concern in the production of first-rate works ... There are no bargains in art,' so it is hardly surprising that his relationship with Heathcoat Amory, the hunting squire, was an uneasy one.

Why Heathcoat Amory employed Burges in the first place is a mystery. Perhaps he had heard of his dazzling reputation and he may have seen two small commissions lately executed by Burges in the West Country (which have not survived). The first was a table and overmantel designed for Colonel Lygon Somers Cocks in 1858–62 at Treverbyn Vean, his new house near Liskeard. The second was the remodelling of a house named 'The Daison' near Torquay for Mr W. J. Potts-Chatto in 1865–6. A more plausible theory is that it was Heathcoat Amory's wife who chose such a colour-ful architect. Henrietta came from an interesting family related by marriage to such distinguished Victorians as William Wilberforce, the slavery abolitionist, Cardinal Manning, the Archbishop of Westminster, and, significantly, the 2nd Lord Carrington of Gayhurst, Buckinghamshire, a house remodelled by Burges in the late 1850s and early 1860s. Burges compiled a brief diary abstract for each year of his life after 1834. In

William Burges lived his medieval dreams

1860, amongst a list of 34 persons with whom he came in contact is the name 'Unwin', perhaps a reference to a member of Henrietta's family. In any event, in 1870, when Burges was busily engaged at Knightshayes, there is another brief entry, 'Gave bracelet to Mrs Amory', indicating their friendly relationship.

The notebooks in which Burges made brief random jottings about his work offer the oc-casional clue of progress made at Knightshayes, while a number of surviving architectural drawings from the Knightshayes Estate Office provide useful evidence. Apart from two major modifications, the exterior of the house was built very nearly as Burges first proposed. The modifications were the

Burges's design for the garden front

reduction of the great tower designed over the staircase on the north-west corner, and changing the axis of the Billiard Room from east–west to north–south.

On Saturday, 17 April 1869 the foundation stone was laid amid 'considerable mirth and festivity', according to the *Tiverton Gazette*:

The elite of the town and neighbourhood had received invitations to be present and it being known that those of the humbler class would be just as welcome, on Saturday afternoon hundreds might have been seen dressed in their holiday attire, and wending their way towards the beautiful spot, which in future is to be marked by a no less handsome than costly mansion, of which the cornerstone was then about to be laid.

This act was performed 'very intelligently and prettily' by Sir John's four-year-old son Ian, who used a silver trowel to conceal copies of local newspapers, a lemonade bottle and several coins beneath the inscribed stone (it can still be seen on the south front). Refreshments were then served and the *Gazette* observed 'over a hundred workmen who were most vigorously engaged in attacking roast beef and plum pudding'. A hymn was specially composed for the occasion:

Architect of both creations
Not yet is thy word fulfilled
Pour thy Spirit on the nations
Build us up while we build.

The builders were Messrs Fatcher & Son of Salisbury, who were not only the cheapest of nine firms to tender for the job, but who also worked at remarkable speed. By the beginning of 1870 the roof line had been reached and gargoyles were being carved at £2 a piece, whilst inside the Hall, William Hine, a marble mason from Teignmouth, was installing highly polished Devonshire marble columns.

In July that year a perspective view of the house was published in the *Architect* with the information that the carcass was contracted for £14,080,

The Winter Smoking Room at Cardiff Castle, Burges's most elaborate Gothic Revival commission. If he had had his way, Knightshayes would have looked like this

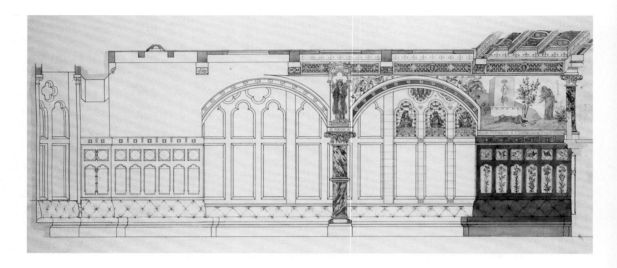

Burges's design for the Drawing Room

excluding the cost of facing stone, cast-iron casements 'and sundry other things', so that 'the actual cost will be something more'. This last observation was a rash understatement, because the climax of Burges's design was reserved for the interior, which he envisaged as a sort of medieval fairyland.

The full extent of his formidable imagination was unleashed on the project, of which tragically little was completed and even less survives. Fortunately, Burges bound his drawings for the scheme into a great album which he presented to the Heathcoat Amorys in November 1873, and this unique document remains in the house. It contains 57 pages of meticulous watercolours depicting every detail from the parquet floors to the painted ceilings, re-creating the sort of medieval interior which Burges so admired:

We should find the ceiling boarded, with paintings on it, generally stars on a green ground; sometimes painted subjects, introduced either in circles or as heads in a border: The walls, if the apartment is a simple one, are simply white, with a pattern in red lines, after the fashion of masonry ... a floriated border running immediately below the ceiling, if ... the apartment is a rich one, the walls have an imitation curtain up to a curtain height, and then picture subjects above. There were two distinct sorts of these; one, where the work was done 'decently' without gold and azure, in fact in lampblack, red and yellow

ochre ... and the other, in full and brilliant colours, with burnished gold ornaments ... But the great feature of our medieval chamber is the furniture; this in a rich apartment, would be covered with paintings, both ornaments and subjects; it not only did its duty as furniture, but spoke and told a story ....

Sadly, it was not to be. The details of what happened are not recorded, but the Heathcoat Amorys probably recoiled at the lavish splendour of the scheme, and the cost. Family tradition relates that on returning from abroad the Heathcoat Amorys were unnerved by the drawings. Moreover, as the late Sir John explained, 'My grandfather was not a very rich man. He knew what he could afford and Burges' final plans came to a lot more!' The last dated drawing is that of 1 July 1875, by which time, although not complete, the house was habitable, since a house-warming party that lasted a week had been held in 1872.

Guests assembled on Monday, 22 January. On Tuesday the gentlemen went shooting. On Wednesday the sportsmen and 'a goodly sprinkling of the fair sex' hunted with Mr Amory's pack of harriers, followed by a dance in 'the spacious ball room thrown open to receive the elite of the county.... Having made this pleasing sacrifice to terpsichore, the following day was devoted to the sister muse of comedy and some excellent charades were acted ... under the able management of Sir Stafford Northcote'. On Friday proceedings were brought to a close by another ball, to which 250 townspeople and neighbouring farmers were invited. The *Tiverton Gazette* recalled, 'Quadrilles and Lancers, Schottisches and Polkers, Reels and Caledonians were played in rapid succession and the sumptuous supper room was amply appreciated, providing strength to dance on until daybreak when the National Anthem followed by ringing cheers for Mr and Mrs Heathcoat Amory signalled the guests' departure.'

It is uncertain what the interior of the house looked like at the time of these celebrations in 1872, when clearly building work was still going on. Burges preferred to follow a timetable at the decorating stage – starting with stone-carving, then wood-carving followed by installing stained glass, painting, and finally introducing furniture, carpets and curtains, in that order. Potentially it was a ruinously extravagant programme, and only at Cardiff Castle and nearby Castell Coch, where the

J. D. Crace's design for the Drawing Room fireplace (now gone)

immensely wealthy and eccentric Lord Bute could afford Burges, are domestic interiors by the architect still to be seen unadulterated by compromise. At Knightshayes only the stone- and wood-carving were ever made to Burges's specification. In his place a cheaper and more fashionable decorator was employed in 1874 to finish the work. His name was John Dibblee Crace.

JOHN DIBBLEE CRACE

Crace's credentials were impeccable. He was the fifth generation in a dynasty of architectural decorators who dominated the field throughout the eighteenth and nineteenth centuries. During that period the London firm of Messrs Crace secured many important decorating commissions, including Carlton House, Covent Garden Opera House, Brighton Pavilion, Windsor Castle, the Houses of Parliament, the Crystal Palace and Chatsworth.

The extent of Crace's work at Knightshayes is known from surviving drawings, now in the Victoria & Albert Museum. These date from 1875 until 1882, when doors and fireplaces were still being fitted, fifteen years after Burges had first drawn up his plans for the house, and about ten years after the Heathcoat Amorys had moved in. Crace's work was, to some extent, governed by the interiors designed by his predecessor but, although colourful, it never displayed the robust fantasy that distinguished Burges's unique style. Crace's decoration was more delicate and sometimes fussy; certainly, he was 'safer' than Burges.

EDWARDIAN ADDITIONS AND THE TWENTIETH CENTURY

By 1885 the Heathcoat Amory household had grown with the addition of six children, and another firm of architects, Ernest George & Peto, was employed to alter the service wing to the east of the main block by adding a third floor incorporating nursery bedrooms. George had already established himself as a competent and successful country house architect, whose most recent creation at Stoodleigh was less than five miles to the north of Knightshayes. His nursery plans never materialised, but in 1902, in association with his new partner, Alfred Yates, he returned to build the Smoking Room on the west side of the house, the last major building campaign at Knightshayes.

In 1914 Sir John Heathcoat Amory died. Despite his years as an MP, the obituaries make no mention of his political career nor his remarkable house. The sporting journal *Baily's Magazine* summed him up: 'He represented a type of man whose value in country life cannot be over-estimated'. He was succeeded by his son Sir Ian, who took a greater interest in the family business than his father, making several important innovations including the introduction of pensions and profit-

sharing schemes for his employees and opening a sales office in New York. Sir Ian also continued the family tradition of hunting, and on one memorable occasion he and his four sons all rode in the same point-to-point race. It was as a result of a hunting accident that he died in 1931.

His eldest son, Sir John, succeeded him and not only successfully developed the business but also enhanced the interest of Knightshayes with his collections of exceptionally fine Old Master paintings and maiolica, which are still displayed in the house. Sir John's brother Derick was active too in the family business, but in 1945 he embarked on a political career, first as MP for Tiverton and culminating in his appointment as Chancellor of the Exchequer in the Macmillan government in 1958. On his retirement from politics in 1960, he was created a Viscount, and a short but useful period of service as High Commissioner in Canada completed his public career. Lord Amory died in 1981, but in 1983 the family was again represented in Parliament by a nephew of Sir John and Lord Amory, David Heathcoat Amory, who remains the Conservative MP for Wells.

Sir John was a keen sportsman and through their mutual interest in golf he met and, in 1937, married Joyce Wethered, who was once described as 'the greatest lady golfer of all time'. During the 1920s she won the British Ladies Open Championship on four occasions and the English Ladies Open on five. Following Sir John's death in 1972, Knightshayes was left to the National Trust, and Lady Heathcoat Amory moved into the former service wing.

Between the wars and during the 1950s, alterations were made to the house at a time when the appreciation of Victorian art and architecture was at its nadir. Ceilings, fireplaces, screens and bookcases were removed, but happily not all was destroyed. It is the Trust's policy to restore these nineteenth-century features of the house in so far as the evidence of old photographs, architectural drawings and salvaged materials survives, and money allows.

Bobby Jones described Joyce Wethered's swing as the best he had ever seen. In 1937 she married Sir John Heathcoat Amory, 3rd Bt